THE BOOK OF
SAUCES
Volume 2

THE BOOK OF
SAUCES
VOLUME 2

ANNE SHEASBY

PHOTOGRAPHED BY
PATRICK McLEAVEY

HPBooks

ANOTHER BEST SELLING VOLUME FROM HPBOOKS

HPBooks
Published by The Berkley Publishing Group
A division of Penguin Putnam Inc.
375 Hudson Street
New York, NY 10014

Copyright © 2002 by Salamander Books Ltd.
By arrangement with Salamander Books Ltd.

A member of Chrysalis Books plc
Project managed by: Stella Caldwell
Editor: Madeline Weston
Photographer: Patrick McLeavey
Designer: Sue Storey
Home Economist: Alex Winsor

All rights reserved. This book, or parts thereof, may not be reproduced in any form without permission.

Notice: The information contained in this book is true and complete to the best of our knowledge. All recommendations are made without any guarantees on the part of the author or the publisher. The author and publisher disclaim all liability in connection with the use of this information.

First edition: April 2002

Visit our website at www.penguinputnam.com

This book has been cataloged with the Library of Congress

ISBN 1-55788-385-8

Printed and bound in Spain

10 9 8 7 6 5 4 3 2 1

CONTENTS

FOREWORD 7

INTRODUCTION 8

HOME-MADE STOCKS 12

BASIC & CLASSIC SAUCES 16

SAUCES FOR MEAT & POULTRY 34

SAUCES FOR FISH & SEAFOOD 44

SAUCES FOR VEGETABLES 54

SALSAS & RELISHES 62

MARINADES & PASTES 72

SWEET SAUCES & COULIS 79

INDEX 96

FOREWORD

Sauces provide the finishing touch to many dishes, enhancing the flavor of food and transforming it into something really special. They are very versatile and can be served with a wide variety of foods and dishes.

The New Book of Sauces is an inspirational collection of tempting recipes suitable for all kinds of foods and for all occasions. We include many basic and classic sauces, as well as flavorful savory sauces, tempting sweet sauces and coulis, creative salsas and relishes, and tasty marinades and pastes.

In this book, you will discover a mouth-watering selection of recipes, both sweet and savory, all of which combine a whole range of different ingredients that are widely and readily available.

Many of these sauces are quick and simple to make, so, why not try some of these delicious recipes and add that special finishing touch to your own dishes?

INTRODUCTION

Sauces are an essential part of every cook's selection of tried and trusted recipes. A good sauce has the ability to turn something plain or ordinary into something special. A sauce may be thick or thin, smooth or chunky, and a flavorful sweet or savory sauce can help to create an everyday meal that is both delicious and memorable. The flavor of many basic sauces can also be varied with the addition of one or more ingredients selected from a whole array of foods.

Some sauces are available commercially in various forms including chilled fresh sauces, bottled or canned sauces, or dry packet mixes, which are combined with liquids such as water, stock, or milk to make a sauce.

In this book, we include an extensive collection of home-made stocks, basic and classic sauces, sauces ideal for transforming foods such as meat, poultry, fish, or vegetables, and sweet sauces, as well as salsas, relishes, marinades, and pastes.

At the end of each recipe, we give some serving suggestions, as well as the quantity or number of servings each recipe makes. Some recipes also include additional ideas for ingredient variations to change the flavor of the basic recipe to suit your own tastes.

HOME-MADE STOCKS

Good home-made stocks add a much better flavor to many savory sauces and it is well worth the small amount of effort it takes to make your own stock. Home-made stocks freeze well and come in handy when you are short of time.

These days, a wide and improved range of stock products is available in our supermarkets and stores. Ready-made stocks such as chilled fresh stocks are widely available and provide a good alternative, if you don't have time to make your own. Stock cubes or bouillon powder are a further

alternative, but they tend to be stronger and more salty in flavor, so should be used sparingly.

TYPES OF SAUCE

A good sauce will complement and enhance the food it is served with and should never overpower the flavor of the dish. Many sauces are simple to make and take a short amount of time, and just a little patience, to create something delicious.

There are several types of sauce including roux-based, brown, or emulsified sauces, fruit or vegetable-based sauces, purées or coulis, gravies, flavored butters, sweet sauces for desserts, salsas, relishes, marinades, or pastes. Recipes for all these types are included in this book.

VOLUME 2

ROUX-BASED SAUCES
Roux-based sauces are based on equal quantities of butter and flour that are cooked together. The butter is melted, then the flour is stirred in and this mixture is known as the 'roux'. The roux is cooked for varying lengths of time depending on the recipe, for example, for a classic white sauce the roux is cooked but not colored, whereas for a brown sauce the roux is cooked for longer until it becomes brown. Liquid is then gradually stirred into the roux and the sauce is then heated, while stirring, until it has thickened.

EMULSIFIED SAUCES
There are two types of emulsified sauce—those based on a butter emulsion (such as hollandaise or béarnaise) or on a cold emulsion of oil and egg yolks (such as mayonnaise or aioli). With emulsified sauces such as hollandaise or beurre blanc, a reduction of the liquid during cooking gives a more intense flavor to the sauce, which is enriched and thickened with the addition of butter or eggs.

FRUIT & VEGETABLE SAUCES & COULIS
Fruit or vegetable-based sauces are very popular and create a whole variety of flavors to accompany a wide range of foods. Fresh fruit coulis are

made by simply puréeing and sieving one or more fresh fruits such as raspberries, apricots or mixed berries, to make a pouring sauce. This creates a range of delicious fruit sauces to accompany desserts such as ice cream or yogurt ice, meringues, fresh fruit, or fruit tartlets.

SALSAS & RELISHES
Salsas and relishes are a combination of finely chopped ingredients, tossed together with other flavorings, to form a delicious and flavorful sauce. They are simple to make and the ingredients used can be varied a great deal to

create a good range of tempting and interesting flavors.

Salsas and relishes provide a tasty accompaniment to many dishes and are excellent served with grilled or char-grilled meats, poultry, fish, or vegetables.

MARINADES & PASTES

Marinades and pastes are an ideal way of adding flavor to meat, poultry, and fish, and occasionally to some vegetables. Marinades or pastes are highly flavored mixtures of ingredients that heighten the flavor of meat, poultry, or fish and often tenderize the meat as well.

Meat, poultry, or fish is added to the marinade or paste and turned or brushed to coat it all over. It is then left to soak or stand for 1 hour or more, depending on the recipe.

The food is then removed from the marinade or paste and cooked. Sometimes the marinade may then be used for basting the food during cooking to prevent it from drying out. On occasions the marinade may be reduced or thickened separately to make a sauce, otherwise it is simply discarded. Marinades are particularly good for use when grilling or broiling meat and poultry.

THICKENING SAUCES

Sauces may be thickened towards the end of cooking in various ways. Cornstarch or arrowroot may be blended with a little water or cold liquid, then added to the sauce and heated, while stirring, until the sauce boils and thickens. Beurre manié (equal quantities of butter and flour are kneaded together then gradually added to hot stock) is another thickener that is added towards the end of the preparation time.

USEFUL EQUIPMENT

Small heavy saucepans are ideal to use when making sauces as they ensure slow, even cooking, which is important for many sauces.

A good balloon whisk is a useful tool to have, particularly when making smooth sauces. A whisk will help prevent lumps forming in the sauce as well as ensuring a smooth, even result. If the sauce does not require whisking, a basic wooden spoon is ideal for sauce-making.

When sieving sauces, such as fruit purées to make coulis, a nylon sieve is very helpful. Use a nylon sieve rather than a metal sieve, especially when sieving fruits or acidic foods, as a metal sieve may impart a little metallic

blender or food processor will help to prevent curdling or separation of the ingredients, which can sometimes occur with this type of recipe.

If a roux-based sauce becomes lumpy, simply whisk or beat it briskly until it becomes smooth. If this doesn't work, you can try sieving the sauce or, alternatively, a blender or food processor can be used to process the sauce until smooth.

If an emulsified sauce shows signs of curdling, it may be rescued by adding an ice cube to the sauce and whisking thoroughly until smooth.

To reduce the risk of curdling when making an egg custard sauce or crème Anglaise, add 1 teaspoon cornstarch to the egg yolks and sugar. Once the custard has thickened, cook the sauce gently for a little longer to make sure the taste of the cornstarch disappears.

If an egg custard sauce shows signs of curdling or separating, strain it into a clean, cold bowl, add a few ice cubes, and whisk briskly to reduce the temperature of the custard, which should become smooth once again.

flavor or occasionally slight discoloration to the food being sieved, which then may spoil the flavor.

A small blender or food processor can be a useful piece of equipment to have when making some types of sauce. It may simply be used to chop ingredients finely for a sauce or paste, or to purée a sauce to make it smoother and more palatable.

RESCUING LUMPY OR CURDLED SAUCES

When making emulsified sauces such as hollandaise or mayonnaise, a

SERVING SAUCES

Some sauces are best served hot, others are best served cold, while some may be served either way. If serving a thickened sauce cold, such as an egg custard sauce, once it is made, cover the top surface closely with damp waxed paper, to prevent a skin forming as the sauce cools. This also applies to sauces that are made in advance, and are to be reheated later when required.

CHICKEN STOCK

1 meaty chicken carcass
1 onion, sliced
2 carrots, sliced
2 stalks celery, chopped
2 bay leaves
salt and freshly ground black pepper

Break or chop chicken carcass into pieces and place in a large saucepan. Add prepared vegetables, bay leaves, seasoning, and 7½ cups cold water and stir to mix.

Bring slowly to a boil, reduce the heat, then partially cover the pan and simmer gently for about 2 hours. From time to time, skim off and discard any scum and fat that rises to the surface.

Strain the stock through a fine sieve into a bowl, adjust the seasoning, then set aside to cool quickly. Use immediately, or cover and chill in the refrigerator for up to 3 days. Remove and discard any fat from the surface of the stock and use the stock as required.

Makes about 3 cups

VARIATIONS: Use 1 meaty turkey carcass in place of chicken. Use 2 leeks or 6 shallots, in place of onion. This stock may be frozen in covered container(s) for up to 3 months.

VOLUME 2

MEAT STOCK

1lb stewing beef or shoulder of lamb, diced
1lb beef or lamb bones
6 shallots or 1 large onion, sliced
2 carrots, sliced
1 turnip, chopped
2 stalks celery, sliced
1 fresh bouquet garni
salt and freshly ground black pepper

Preheat the oven to 425F (220C). Put meat and bones in a roasting pan and bake in the oven for about 30 minutes, or until well browned, turning occasionally.

Transfer the meat, bones and juices to a large saucepan and add 7½ cups cold water. Add the prepared vegetables, bouquet garni, and seasoning, and stir to mix. Bring slowly to a boil, reduce the heat, then partially cover the pan and simmer gently for about 2 hours. From time to time, skim off and discard any scum and fat that rises to the surface.

Strain the stock through a fine sieve into a bowl, adjust the seasoning, then set aside to cool quickly. Use immediately or cover and chill in the refrigerator for up to 3 days. Remove and discard any fat from the surface of the stock and use the stock as required.

Makes about 3 cups

VARIATIONS: Use 4oz diced rutabaga in place of turnip. Use 1-2 bay leaves in place of bouquet garni. This stock may be frozen in covered container(s) for up to 3 months.

FISH STOCK

2¼lb fish bones and trimmings
1 large onion, chopped
1 large carrot, sliced
3 stalks celery, chopped
1 bay leaf
small bunch of fresh parsley
salt and freshly ground black pepper

Wash the fish trimmings and put them in a large saucepan with the prepared vegetables, bay leaf, parsley, and seasoning.

Add 4½ cups cold water and stir to mix. Bring slowly to a boil, reduce the heat, then partially cover the pan and simmer gently for about 30 minutes. From time to time, skim off and discard any scum that rises to the surface.

Remove any large bones, then strain the stock through a fine sieve into a bowl, adjust seasoning, and set aside to cool. Use immediately or cover and chill in the refrigerator for up to 2 days. Use as required.

Makes about 3¾ cups

VARIATIONS: Use 6 shallots or 2 leeks in place of onion. Use 1 large parsnip, thickly sliced, in place of carrot. This stock may be frozen in covered container(s) for up to 1 month.

VEGETABLE STOCK

1 large onion, chopped
2 leeks, washed and sliced
2 carrots, sliced
4 stalks celery, chopped
6oz rutabaga, diced
1 parsnip, thickly sliced
1 fresh bouquet garni
8 black peppercorns
½ teaspoon salt

Put all the prepared vegetables, bouquet garni, black peppercorns, and salt in a large saucepan. Add 7½ cups cold water and stir to mix.

Bring slowly to a boil, reduce the heat, then partially cover the pan and simmer gently for about 1 hour. From time to time, skim off and discard any scum that rises to the surface.

Strain the stock through a fine sieve into a bowl, adjust the seasoning, then set aside to cool. Use immediately or cover and chill in the refrigerator for up to 3 days. Use as required.

Makes about 5 cups

VARIATIONS: Use turnip in place of rutabaga. Use 1-2 bay leaves in place of bouquet garni. This stock may be frozen in covered container(s) for up to 3 months.

THE BOOK OF SAUCES

BASIC WHITE SAUCE

1 tablespoon butter
2 tablespoons all-purpose flour
1¼ cups milk
salt and freshly ground black pepper

Melt the butter in a small saucepan, stir in the flour, and cook, stirring, for 1 minute. Remove the pan from the heat and gradually whisk in the milk.

Return to the heat and bring slowly to a boil, stirring or whisking until the sauce is thickened and smooth. Simmer gently for 2 minutes, stirring. Season to taste with salt and pepper. Serve with cooked meat, poultry, fish, or vegetables.

Makes about 1¼ cups
Serves 4

VARIATION: For a Thick/Coating Sauce, increase the butter to 2 tablespoons and flour to ¼ cup.

FOR A BLENDED WHITE SAUCE
Measure 1¼ cups milk. Blend 5 teaspoons cornstarch with a little of the milk in a bowl to form a smooth paste. Heat remaining milk in a small saucepan with ½ oz of butter, until boiling. Pour the hot milk on to the cornstarch mixture, stirring continuously. Return the mixture to the saucepan and bring slowly to a boil, stirring, until the sauce thickens. Simmer gently for 2-3 minutes, stirring. Season to taste with salt and pepper. Serve.

WHITE SAUCE VARIATIONS

CHEESE (MORNAY) SAUCE
Follow the recipe for Basic White Sauce. Before seasoning, remove the pan from the heat, and stir in ½ cup finely grated mature Cheddar or Gruyère cheese and 1 teaspoon Dijon mustard. Add salt and freshly ground black pepper to taste. Serve with cooked fish, ham, vegetables, or egg dishes.

PARSLEY SAUCE
Follow the recipe for Basic White Sauce. Stir in 2-3 tablespoons chopped fresh parsley just before serving. Serve with cooked fish, ham, bacon, or vegetables.

ONION SAUCE
Finely chop 1 large onion and sauté in ¼ cup butter for 10-15 minutes, or until softened. Follow the recipe for Basic White Sauce. Stir the sautéed onion into the cooked white sauce just before serving. Serve with cooked meat, poultry, or fish.

BÉCHAMEL SAUCE

1¼ cups milk
1 small onion or shallot, cut in half
1 small carrot, thickly sliced
1 bay leaf
6 black peppercorns
a few fresh parsley stalks
1 tablespoon butter
2 tablespoons all-purpose flour
salt and freshly ground black pepper
freshly grated nutmeg, to taste (optional)

Pour the milk into a small saucepan and add onion or shallot, carrot, bay leaf, black peppercorns, and parsley stalks.

Bring almost to a boil, then remove the pan from the heat, cover, and leave to infuse for 30 minutes. Strain into a jug, reserving the milk and discarding the contents of the sieve. Melt butter in a separate small saucepan, stir in flour, and cook, stirring, for 1 minute. Remove the pan from the heat and gradually whisk in infused milk.

Return to the heat and bring slowly to a boil, whisking until the sauce is thickened and smooth. Simmer gently for 2 minutes, stirring. Season with salt and pepper and nutmeg, if using. Serve with fish, broiled or grilled chicken, or cooked vegetables.

Makes about 1¼ cups
Serves 4

VARIATION: For a thicker sauce, increase the butter to 2 tablespoons and flour to ¼ cup.

QUICK TOMATO SAUCE

1 tablespoon olive oil
1 onion, finely chopped
2 cloves garlic, crushed
2 (14oz) cans chopped tomatoes
2 tablespoons tomato paste
2 tablespoons medium-dry sherry
½ teaspoon caster sugar
salt and freshly ground black pepper

Heat the oil in a saucepan, add onion and garlic, and cook gently for 8-10 minutes, stirring occasionally, until softened.

Add the tomatoes with their juice, tomato paste, sherry, sugar, and salt and pepper, and mix well. Bring to a boil, then cook gently, uncovered, for about 25 minutes, stirring occasionally, until the sauce is thick and pulpy. Adjust the seasoning and serve. Serve with cooked pasta, meat, poultry, fish, vegetables, or egg dishes.

Makes about 3½ cups
Serves 4-6

VARIATIONS: Stir 1 tablespoon chopped fresh mixed herbs into the sauce just before serving. Use white or red wine in place of sherry.

COOK'S TIP: Once cooked, this sauce may be cooled slightly, then puréed in a blender or food processor until smooth. Reheat gently before serving.

ESPAGNOLE (BROWN) SAUCE

2 tablespoons butter
1 slice bacon, chopped
1 small onion, finely chopped
1 small carrot, finely chopped
1 stalk celery, finely chopped
2oz mushrooms, finely chopped
¼ cup all-purpose flour
2 cups meat stock (see page 13)
2 tablespoons tomato paste
1 fresh bouquet garni
salt and freshly ground black pepper

Melt butter in a saucepan, add the bacon, and cook for 2-3 minutes, stirring.

Add onion, carrot, celery, and mushrooms and cook gently for 6-8 minutes, stirring occasionally, until softened. Stir in flour and cook, stirring, until the mixture is brown. Remove the pan from the heat and gradually whisk in the stock. Return to the heat and bring slowly to a boil, stirring or whisking until the sauce is thickened. Add the tomato paste, bouquet garni, and seasoning. Partially cover the pan and simmer gently for about 1 hour, stirring occasionally.

Strain the sauce into a clean pan and discard the contents of the sieve. Reheat gently and adjust the seasoning before serving. Serve with cooked red meats, game, or variety meats.

Makes about 1¼ cups
Serves 4

VARIATION: Use 2 shallots in place of onion.

RÉMOULADE SAUCE

2 teaspoons capers, drained
3 cocktail gherkins, drained
1 anchovy fillet
⅔ cup mayonnaise (see page 30)
1 teaspoon Dijon mustard
2 teaspoons finely chopped fresh tarragon
2 teaspoons chopped fresh parsley
salt and freshly ground black pepper

Finely chop the capers, gherkins, and anchovy fillet, and place in a bowl.

Add the mayonnaise, mustard, tarragon, and parsley, and mix well.

Season to taste with salt and pepper. Serve with cooked cold meat and poultry, shellfish, and hard-boiled eggs.

Makes about scant 1 cup
Serves 4-6

BEURRE BLANC

3 tablespoons white wine
3 tablespoons white wine vinegar
1 shallot, finely chopped
1 cup butter, chilled and cut into small cubes
salt and freshly ground black pepper
lemon juice
1 tablespoon chopped fresh parsley (optional)

Put white wine, wine vinegar, and shallot in a small saucepan, bring to a boil, and boil until reduced to about 2 tablespoons. Strain and return to the pan.

Over a low heat, gradually whisk in the chilled butter, piece by piece. The sauce should become pale, thick and creamy as the butter melts. Remove the pan from the heat to prevent overheating.

Season to taste with salt and pepper and a squeeze of lemon juice. Stir in parsley, if using. Serve with broiled, grilled or poached fish or poultry.

Makes about scant 1 cup
Serves 4-6

VELOUTÉ SAUCE

1½ tablespoons butter
3 tablespoons all-purpose flour
1¼ cups home-made stock (meat, chicken, fish or vegetable stock may be used, see pages 12-15)
2 tablespoons heavy cream
½ teaspoon lemon juice
salt and freshly ground black pepper

Melt butter in a small saucepan, stir in flour, and cook, stirring, for about 2 minutes, until light golden in color.

Remove the pan from the heat and gradually whisk in the stock. Return to the heat and bring slowly to a boil, stirring or whisking until the sauce is thickened and smooth. Simmer gently for 2 minutes, stirring.

Stir in the cream, then stir in the lemon juice and season to taste with salt and pepper. Serve with broiled, grilled or baked fish, poultry or meat, or cooked vegetables.

Makes about 1¼ cups
Serves 4

HOLLANDAISE

3 tablespoons white wine vinegar
6 black peppercorns
1 slice of onion
1 bay leaf
1 blade mace
2 egg yolks
½ cup butter, at room temperature, diced
salt and freshly ground black pepper
lemon juice, to taste

Put vinegar in a small saucepan with peppercorns, onion, bay leaf, and mace. Bring to a boil and simmer until reduced to 1 tablespoon. Remove from heat; set aside.

Put egg yolks in a heatproof bowl with 1 tablespoon of the butter and a pinch of salt, and beat together using a balloon whisk. Strain the reduced vinegar into the egg mixture and stir to mix. Place the bowl over a pan of barely simmering water and whisk egg mixture for 3-4 minutes, until pale and beginning to thicken. Gradually whisk in remaining butter, one piece at a time, until mixture begins to thicken and emulsify. Make sure each piece of butter is incorporated into the sauce before adding the next piece.

Remove the bowl from the heat. Whisk for 1 minute. Adjust the seasoning and add lemon juice to taste. Serve immediately with poached fish or shellfish, or cooked vegetables such as asparagus or globe artichokes.

Makes about ⅔ cup
Serves 4-6

COOK'S TIP: Hollandaise will curdle if allowed to overheat. If it begins to curdle, add an ice cube and whisk well; the sauce should recombine.

BARBECUE SAUCE

3 tablespoons butter
1 onion, finely chopped
⅔ cup tomato juice
2 tablespoons red wine vinegar
1 tablespoon Worcestershire sauce
1 tablespoon light soft brown sugar
2 teaspoons English mustard
1 tablespoon tomato paste
salt and freshly ground black pepper

Melt the butter in a small saucepan, add the onion, and cook gently for 8-10 minutes, stirring occasionally, until softened.

Add tomato juice, vinegar, Worcestershire sauce, sugar, mustard, tomato paste, and seasoning and mix well. Bring to a boil, then simmer, uncovered, for 10-15 minutes, stirring occasionally.

If you would like a smoother sauce, allow the sauce to cool slightly, then purée in a blender or food processor. Reheat gently before serving. Serve with broiled or grilled meat such as steaks, chops, chicken portions, sausages, or burgers.

Makes about 1¼ cups
Serves 4-6

VARIATION: Use 4 shallots in place of onion. Use tomato paste in place of tomato juice.

FRESH CRANBERRY SAUCE

1 small orange
2 cups fresh cranberries
½ cup superfine or light soft brown sugar
1-2 tablespoons ruby port (optional)

Finely grate the rind from the orange and squeeze the juice.

Place the cranberries in a saucepan with the orange juice, sugar, and ⅔ cup water. Bring to a boil, then cook gently, uncovered, for 20-30 minutes, stirring occasionally, until the cranberries are soft. Remove the pan from the heat. Using a slotted spoon, remove half the cranberries and place in a bowl. Purée the remaining cranberries and juices in a blender or food processor.

Add the cranberry purée to the reserved cranberries in the bowl, then stir in the orange rind and port, if using, mixing well. Allow to cool, then serve warm or cold with hot or cold roast turkey or pork.

Makes about 1¼ cups
Serves 6-8

MINT SAUCE

small bunch of fresh mint, stalks removed
2 teaspoons superfine sugar
1 tablespoon boiling water
1 tablespoon white wine vinegar

Wash the mint leaves and shake them dry. Finely chop the mint leaves, then place them in a bowl with the sugar.

Pour on the boiling water, stir to mix, then set aside for 5 minutes, or until the sugar has dissolved.

Add the vinegar and stir to mix. Set aside and leave to stand for 1-2 hours before serving. Serve with roast lamb.

Makes about 3 tablespoons
Serves 4

AIOLI

2 pasteurized egg yolks
1 tablespoon lemon juice
4 cloves garlic, crushed
½ teaspoon salt
freshly ground black pepper
1¼ cups light olive or sunflower oil

Put the egg yolks, lemon juice, garlic, salt, and black pepper to taste in a small blender or food processor and blend for about 20 seconds, until pale and creamy.

With the motor running, gradually add the oil, pouring it in a slow, steady stream through the feeder tube, until the mayonnaise is thick and creamy.

Adjust the seasoning, then cover and chill until required. Store in a covered container in the refrigerator for up to 2 days. Serve with cooked cold fish, chicken, meat, shellfish, salads, or hard-boiled eggs.

Makes about 1¼ cups
Serves 6

WARNING: It is possible that raw eggs may contain salmonella. They should not be served to anyone with a serious illness or compromised immune system.

CLASSIC PESTO

2oz basil leaves
¼ cup pine nuts
1 clove garlic, crushed
scant ½ cup olive oil
½ cup finely grated fresh Parmesan cheese
salt and freshly ground black pepper

Put the basil leaves, pine nuts, garlic, and olive oil in a small blender or food processor and blend to form a fairly smooth paste.

Add the Parmesan and salt and pepper, and process briefly to mix. Store in a covered jar in the refrigerator for up to 1 week. Serve with pasta, broiled or grilled chicken, or poached fish.

Makes about generous 1 cup
Serves 4-6

COOK'S TIP: Or, place basil, pine nuts, and garlic in a mortar with a little oil and pound together. Gradually work in remaining oil, then stir in cheese and seasoning.

FLAVOR VARIATIONS: For Red Pesto, reduce the quantity of pine nuts to 2 tablespoons and add 2oz sun-dried tomatoes in oil, drained and chopped, and 1 tablespoon tomato paste with the basil. Use pecorino cheese in place of Parmesan, if liked.

For Cilantro Pesto, replace the basil with fresh cilantro and omit the cheese.

For Arugula Pesto, replace the basil with fresh arugula and replace the pine nuts with blanched almonds.

MAYONNAISE

2 pasteurized egg yolks
1 teaspoon Dijon mustard
1 tablespoon lemon juice or white wine vinegar
pinch superfine sugar
½ teaspoon salt
freshly ground black pepper
1¼ cups light olive or sunflower oil

Put the egg yolks, mustard, lemon juice or vinegar, sugar, salt, and black pepper to taste in a small blender or food processor.

Blend for about 20 seconds, until smooth, pale, and creamy.

With the motor running, gradually add the oil, pouring it through the feeder tube, until the mayonnaise is thick and smooth. Adjust the seasoning, then cover and chill until required, for up to 3 days.

Makes about 1¼ cups
Serves 6

WARNING: It is possible that raw eggs may contain salmonella. They should not be served to anyone with a serious illness or compromised immune system.

MAYONNAISE VARIATIONS

FLAVOR VARIATIONS: For Lemon Mayonnaise, use lemon juice and stir 1½ teaspoons finely grated lemon rind into mayonnaise, just before serving.

For Garlic & Herb Mayonnaise, add 1 crushed clove garlic with the egg yolks. Fold 2 tablespoons chopped fresh mixed herbs (such as chives, parsley, tarragon, and oregano) into mayonnaise just before serving.

For Horseradish Mayonnaise, fold 2 tablespoons hot horseradish sauce into mayonnaise, just before serving.

For Mustard Mayonnaise, fold 2 tablespoons Dijon or grainy mustard into mayonnaise, just before serving.

For Curried Mayonnaise, fold 1-2 tablespoons curry paste into mayonnaise, just before serving.

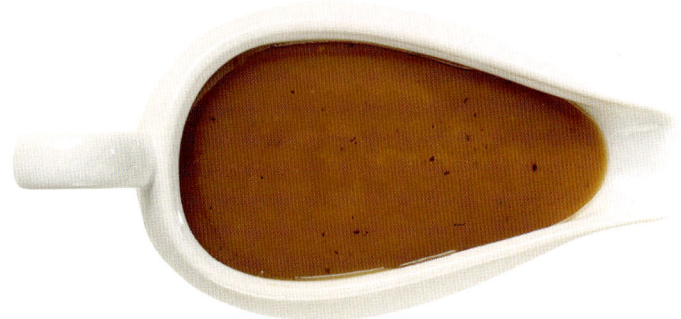

TRADITIONAL GRAVY

2 tablespoons butter
2 tablespoons all-purpose flour
2 shallots, chopped
1¼ cups chicken or meat stock (see pages 12-13) or water from cooking vegetables
1 teaspoon yeast extract
1 teaspoon dried mixed herbs
salt and freshly ground black pepper

Put 1 tablespoon of the butter and all the flour in a small bowl and mix together until well blended to make a paste. Set aside.

Melt the remaining butter in a small saucepan, add the shallots, and cook gently for 8-10 minutes, stirring occasionally, until softened. Stir in the stock or vegetable water, yeast extract, and herbs, and bring to a boil. Reduce the heat, cover and simmer for 5 minutes. Remove the shallots using a slotted spoon and discard them. Bring the liquid back to a boil, then add the paste a little at a time, whisking continuously to blend in well with the liquid, until all the paste has been added.

Continue to cook, whisking, until the gravy thickens. Simmer gently for 5 minutes, stirring. Season to taste. Serve with roast meats such as beef, lamb, pork, or chicken. (Add any juices from the roasted meat to the gravy for extra flavor and color.)

Makes about ¾ cup
Serves 2-4

VARIATION: Replace ¼ cup of the stock with red or white wine, if liked.

BLUE CHEESE SAUCE

1 tablespoon butter
2 shallots, finely chopped
1 stalk celery, finely chopped
2 tablespoons dry sherry
scant 1 cup crème fraiche or heavy cream
3oz blue cheese such as Stilton
  or Gorgonzola, crumbled
1 tablespoon chopped fresh parsley
salt and freshly ground black pepper

Melt the butter in a small saucepan, add the shallots and celery, and cook gently for 10-15 minutes, stirring occasionally, until softened.

Add the sherry and boil until reduced slightly. Add the crème fraiche or heavy cream, bring to a boil, and bubble for about 5 minutes, stirring occasionally, until thickened slightly.

Stir in the blue cheese until melted, then stir in the parsley. Add salt and pepper to taste. Serve with broiled or grilled meat or poultry, such as steaks or chicken portions. This sauce is also good served with cooked vegetables.

Makes about 1⅓ cups
Serves 4

VARIATIONS: Use 1 small onion in place of shallots. Use fresh chives in place of parsley.

HORSERADISH CREAM

⅔ cup heavy cream
2-3 tablespoons grated fresh horseradish
 (depending on taste)
2 teaspoons white wine vinegar
salt and freshly ground black pepper
superfine sugar, to taste

Pour the cream into a bowl and whip until thick.

In a separate bowl, mix the horseradish and vinegar together.

Fold into the whipped cream, then add salt, pepper, and sugar to taste. Cover and chill in the refrigerator until ready to serve. Serve with hot or cold roast beef. This sauce is also good served with cooked fresh or smoked mackerel, or smoked salmon or trout.

Makes about 1 cup
Serves 4-6

VOLUME 2

WILD MUSHROOM SAUCE

2 tablespoons olive oil
3 shallots, finely chopped
2 cloves garlic, crushed
8oz fresh mixed wild mushrooms such as shiitake and oyster mushrooms, sliced
4oz brown mushrooms, sliced
¾ cup dry white wine
⅓ cup hot vegetable stock (see page 15)
scant 1 cup crème fraîche or heavy cream
salt and freshly ground black pepper
2 tablespoons chopped fresh flat-leaf parsley

Heat oil in a saucepan, add shallots and garlic, and cook gently for 8-10 minutes, stirring occasionally, until softened.

Add all the mushrooms and cook for 3-4 minutes, stirring occasionally, until tender. Add the wine, bring to the boil, and boil until reduced by about half. Add the stock, crème fraîche or heavy cream, and salt and pepper, bring to the boil, and bubble for about 5 minutes or until the sauce thickens slightly, stirring occasionally.

Stir in the parsley and serve with grilled, roast, or pan-fried meats and poultry, such as steaks, chops, or chicken or turkey portions.

Makes about 3 cups
Serves 6

VARIATIONS: Use 1 onion in place of the shallots. Use button or closed-cup mushrooms in place of brown mushrooms.

LEMON CAPER SAUCE

2 tablespoons butter
¼ cup all-purpose flour
1¼ cups milk
2 tablespoons capers, drained and chopped
1 tablespoon vinegar from jar of capers
finely grated rind of 1 small lemon
salt and freshly ground black pepper

Melt the butter in a small saucepan, stir in the flour, and cook, stirring, for 1 minute. Remove the pan from the heat and gradually whisk in the milk.

Return to the heat and bring slowly to a boil, stirring or whisking, until the sauce is thickened and smooth. Simmer gently for 2 minutes, stirring.

Stir in the capers, vinegar, and lemon rind, and reheat gently until almost boiling. Season to taste with salt and pepper. Serve with roast or broiled meat such as lamb, pork, or ham. This sauce is also good served with poached or broiled white fish.

Makes about 1 ½ cups
Serves 4

RED WINE (BURGUNDY) SAUCE

2 tablespoons butter
1 small onion, finely chopped
1 clove garlic, crushed
2 tablespoons all-purpose flour
2 teaspoons light brown sugar
1¼ cups burgundy or red wine
1 tablespoon medium-dry sherry
1 teaspoon chopped fresh thyme
salt and freshly ground black pepper

Melt the butter in a small saucepan, add onion and garlic, and cook for 8-10 minutes, stirring, until softened. Stir in flour and sugar, and cook for 1 minute, stirring.

Remove the pan from the heat and gradually whisk in the wine and sherry. Return to the heat and bring slowly to a boil, stirring or whisking continuously, until the sauce is thickened. Simmer gently for 2 minutes, stirring.

Stir in the thyme, and season to taste with salt and pepper. Serve, or, if liked, cool slightly, then purée in a blender or food processor until smooth. Reheat gently before serving. Serve with broiled or pan-fried meat such as steak or lamb.

Makes about 1¼ cups
Serves 4-6

VARIATIONS: Use 2 shallots in place of onion. Use chopped fresh rosemary or oregano in place of thyme.

CREAMY ARTICHOKE SAUCE

3 tablespoons butter
3 shallots, finely chopped
¼ cup all-purpose flour
1¼ cups vegetable stock (see page 15)
⅔ cup heavy cream
14oz can artichoke hearts, drained and chopped
salt and freshly ground black pepper

Melt the butter in a saucepan, add the shallots, and sauté for 6-8 minutes, until softened. Stir in the flour, and cook gently for 1 minute, stirring.

Remove the pan from the heat, gradually whisk in the stock, then stir in the cream. Return to the heat and bring slowly to a boil, stirring or whisking continuously, until the sauce is thickened. Simmer gently for 2 minutes, stirring.

Stir in the artichoke hearts, then reheat gently until hot, stirring. Season to taste with salt and pepper. Serve with broiled or baked chicken or turkey portions. This sauce is also good served with broiled or baked white or oily fish.

Makes about 3 cups
Serves 4-6

VARIATIONS: Use 1 small leek in place of shallots. Use milk in place of vegetable stock.

PEANUT SATAY SAUCE

¾ cup dry-roasted peanuts
1 tablespoon olive oil
1 onion, finely chopped
2 cloves garlic, crushed
1 fresh red chili, cored, seeded, and finely chopped
1in piece fresh root ginger, peeled and finely chopped
14oz can coconut milk
juice of 1 lime
1 tablespoon light soft brown sugar
salt, to taste

Put the peanuts in a blender or food processor and process until they are finely chopped. Set aside.

Heat the oil in a saucepan, add the onion, and sauté for 5 minutes, until softened. Add the garlic, chili, and ginger, and cook for 2 minutes, stirring. Add the onion mixture to the peanuts in the processor, and process briefly to mix.

Transfer the mixture to the saucepan, add the coconut milk, lime juice, and sugar, and mix well. Bring slowly to a boil, then reduce the heat and simmer, uncovered, for 10-15 minutes, or until the sauce is thickened, stirring occasionally. Season to taste with salt, if required. Serve as a dipping sauce with broiled or grilled chicken, beef, lamb, or pork kabobs, or broiled chicken or turkey portions.

Makes about 2¼ cups
Serves 6-8

TARRAGON SAUCE

1½ tablespoons butter
3 tablespoons all-purpose flour
⅔ cup vegetable stock (see page 15)
⅔ cup milk
4 tablespoons heavy cream
1½ teaspoons Dijon mustard
1 tablespoon chopped fresh tarragon
salt and freshly ground black pepper

Melt the butter in a small saucepan, stir in the flour, and cook, stirring, for 1 minute. Remove the pan from the heat and gradually whisk in the stock, milk, and cream.

Return to the heat, and bring slowly to a boil, stirring or whisking until the sauce is thickened and smooth. Simmer gently for 2 minutes, stirring.

Stir in the mustard and tarragon, and season to taste with salt and pepper. Serve with broiled or grilled poultry or meat, such as chicken breasts or lamb cutlets. This sauce is also good served with broiled, baked, or pan-fried white fish.

Makes about 1½ cups
Serves 4

VARIATION: Stir ½ cup finely grated Cheddar cheese into sauce, just before serving, if liked.

PLUM & GINGER SAUCE

1 tablespoon sunflower oil
2 shallots, finely chopped
1 clove garlic, crushed
2 teaspoons grated fresh ginger root
12oz red dessert plums, halved, pitted, and chopped
⅔ cup red wine
2 tablespoons light brown sugar
1 tablespoon brandy (optional)

Heat the oil in a saucepan, add the shallots, garlic, and ginger, and cook gently for 5 minutes, stirring occasionally. Add the plums and sauté for 1 minute, stirring.

Stir in the wine and sugar, and heat gently, stirring, until the sugar has dissolved. Bring slowly to a boil, then reduce the heat, cover, and simmer for about 10 minutes, or until the plums are soft.

Remove the pan from the heat and cool slightly, then purée the mixture in a blender or food processor until smooth. Return the sauce to the rinsed-out pan, and stir in the brandy, if using. Reheat gently until hot. Serve hot or cold with roast or grilled meat such as beef, pork, lamb, or duck.

Makes about 2 cups
Serves 6-8

GREEN PEPPERCORN SAUCE

⅔ cup dry white wine
2 tablespoons brandy
scant 1 cup crème fraîche or heavy cream
1 teaspoon Dijon mustard
1 tablespoon green peppercorns in brine, rinsed and drained
2 tablespoons chopped fresh parsley
salt and freshly ground black pepper

Put the wine and brandy in a small saucepan and bring to a boil. Simmer, uncovered, for about 10 minutes, or until the liquid has reduced by about half.

Whisk the crème fraîche or heavy cream into the sauce, bring slowly to a boil, then bubble for about 10 minutes, or until the sauce is thickened slightly.

Whisk the mustard into the sauce, then stir in the green peppercorns and parsley. Season to taste with salt and pepper. Serve with broiled or pan-fried meat or poultry such as beef, pork, duck, or chicken. This sauce is also good served with broiled or pan-fried white or oily fish.

Makes about 1 cup
Serves 2-4

SPICY THAI DIPPING SAUCE

3 scallions
2 tablespoons light soy sauce
3 tablespoons lemon juice
2 tablespoons medium-hot chili sauce
½ teaspoon Thai 7-spice seasoning
1 tablespoon chopped fresh cilantro
1-2 teaspoons light brown sugar

Finely chop the scallions.

Place the scallions in a small bowl with the soy sauce, lemon juice, chili sauce, and Thai seasoning, and mix well.

Stir in the chopped cilantro. Stir in the sugar to taste. Serve as a dipping sauce with cooked Thai beef, pork, or chicken dishes.

Makes about ⅔ cup
Serves 4

VARIATIONS: Use lime juice in place of lemon juice. Use fish sauce in place of chili sauce.

TOMATO & BASIL SAUCE

1½lb fresh plum tomatoes
1 tablespoon olive oil
1 red onion, finely chopped
2 cloves garlic, crushed
2 stalks celery, finely chopped
4 sun-dried tomatoes in oil, drained and finely chopped
6 tablespoons red wine
1 tablespoon tomato paste
½ teaspoon superfine sugar
salt and freshly ground black pepper
3-4 tablespoons chopped fresh basil

Using a sharp knife, cut a small cross in blossom end of each tomato.

Place the tomatoes in a bowl, cover with boiling water; leave for 30 seconds. Remove using a slotted spoon and plunge into cold water, then drain well. Peel off skins, then halve tomatoes and remove and discard the seeds. Chop flesh and set aside. Heat oil in a saucepan, add onion, garlic and celery, and cook gently for 5 minutes, stirring occasionally. Add chopped tomatoes, sun-dried tomatoes, red wine, tomato paste, sugar, and seasoning, and mix well. Bring to a boil, then reduce the heat, cover, and simmer for 15 minutes, stirring occasionally.

Uncover the pan, increase the heat slightly, and cook for a further 10-15 minutes, stirring occasionally, until the mixture is thick and pulpy. Stir in the chopped basil, and adjust the seasoning to taste. Serve with broiled, baked, or pan-fried white fish such as monkfish, haddock, or mackerel. This sauce is also good served with cooked hot pasta.

Makes about 3 cups
Serves 4-6

WATERCRESS SAUCE

1 bunch of watercress (about 3½oz total weight)
2 tablespoons butter
¼ cup all-purpose flour
1¼ cups fish or vegetable stock (see pages 14-15)
⅔ cup heavy cream
salt and freshly ground black pepper

Trim the watercress, then blanch it in boiling water for 30 seconds. Refresh under cold running water, drain well, and pat dry with absorbent paper towels. Chop finely, then set aside.

Melt the butter in a small saucepan, then stir in the flour and cook gently for 1 minute, stirring. Remove the pan from the heat, and gradually whisk in the stock and cream. Return to the heat and bring slowly to the boil, stirring or whisking continuously, until the sauce is thickened and smooth. Simmer gently for 2 minutes, stirring.

Add the watercress and cook gently for 1 minute, stirring. Season to taste. If you like, allow to cool slightly, then purée in a blender or food processor. Reheat gently. Serve with broiled or baked fish such as salmon or tuna steaks, or trout or mackerel fillets. This sauce is also good served with broiled or baked chicken or turkey.

Makes about 2¼ cups
Serves 4-6

VARIATION: Use milk in place of stock.

— CREAMY MUSHROOM SAUCE —

⅔ cup fish or vegetable stock (see pages 14-15)
1¼ cups heavy cream
3 tablespoons butter
6oz brown mushrooms, sliced
4oz button mushrooms, sliced
1-2 tablespoons chopped fresh mixed herbs such as parsley, chives, and tarragon or cilantro
salt and freshly ground black pepper

Pour the stock and cream into a saucepan. Bring slowly to a boil, then simmer gently until the sauce thickens slightly to a coating consistency, stirring frequently.

Meanwhile, melt the butter in a skillet, add all the mushrooms, and sauté for about 5 minutes, until soft. Increase the heat slightly and cook, stirring frequently, until all the liquid has evaporated.

Add the mushrooms and chopped herbs to the cream sauce and reheat gently, stirring. Season to taste with salt and pepper. Serve with broiled, baked, or poached fish such as cod, monkfish, or salmon. This sauce is also good served with broiled meats or poultry.

Makes about 2¾ cups
Serves 4-6

VARIATIONS: Use closed cup mushrooms in place of brown mushrooms and fresh wild mushrooms in place of button mushrooms.

DILL & MUSTARD SAUCE

scant 1 cup dry white wine
scant 1 cup fish or vegetable stock (see pages 14-15)
scant 1 cup crème fraîche or heavy cream
2 tablespoons wholegrain mustard
2 egg yolks
2 tablespoons chopped fresh dill
salt and freshly ground black pepper

Put the wine and stock in a saucepan, bring to a boil, and boil until reduced by half.

Reduce the heat and stir in the crème fraîche or heavy cream, mustard, egg yolks, and dill. Cook gently, stirring continuously, for about 10 minutes, or until the sauce is thickened slightly. Do not allow the mixture to boil.

Season to taste with salt and pepper. Serve with pan-fried or broiled fish such as plaice, halibut, haddock, or mackerel.

Makes about 1¾ cups
Serves 6

VARIATIONS: Use 2-3 teaspoons hot horseradish sauce or to taste, in place of dill.

AVOCADO SAUCE

1 lime or 1 small lemon
2 ripe avocados
scant 1 cup plain yogurt
scant ½ cup mayonnaise (see page 30)
1 tablespoon chopped fresh chives
salt and freshly ground black pepper

Finely grate the rind and squeeze the juice from the lime.

Peel, halve, and pit the avocados, then roughly chop the flesh. Place the avocado flesh and lime rind and juice in a blender or food processor.

Add the yogurt and mayonnaise and blend until smooth and well mixed. Add the chives and blend briefly to mix. Season to taste with salt and pepper. Serve immediately with broiled or baked fish such as salmon, tuna, or trout, stir-fried jumbo shrimp, or cold cooked seafood such as shrimp.

Makes about 2¾ cups
Serves 6-8

VARIATION: Use parsley in place of chives.

WHITE WINE SAUCE

¾ cup dry white wine
scant 1 cup heavy cream
scant ½ cup fish or vegetable stock
   (see pages 14-15)
1 tablespoon chopped fresh dill (optional)
1 tablespoon chopped fresh parsley
salt and freshly ground black pepper

Pour the wine into a small saucepan, bring to a boil, then boil rapidly until reduced by half.

Stir in the cream and stock, bring to a boil, and simmer for 10-15 minutes, stirring occasionally, until the sauce has thickened slightly.

Remove the pan from the heat and stir in the chopped dill, if using, and chopped parsley. Season to taste with salt and pepper. Serve with broiled, baked, or poached white fish such as plaice, halibut, or lemon sole. This sauce is also good served with broiled or pan-fried chicken or turkey.

Makes about 1¼ cups
Serves 4-6

VARIATION: Use crème fraîche in place of heavy cream.

CREAMY CRAB SAUCE

1½ tablespoons butter
3 tablespoons all-purpose flour
⅔ cup milk
⅔ cup fish or vegetable stock
  (see pages 14-15)
scant ½ cup heavy cream
8oz cooked crabmeat, flaked
2 tablespoons chopped fresh cilantro
salt and freshly ground black pepper

Melt the butter in a small saucepan, then stir in the flour and cook gently for 1 minute, stirring.

Remove the pan from the heat and gradually whisk in the milk, stock, and cream. Return to the heat and bring slowly to a boil, stirring or whisking continuously, until the sauce is thickened and smooth. Simmer gently for 2 minutes, stirring.

Stir in the crabmeat and reheat gently until hot. Stir in the chopped cilantro and season to taste with salt and pepper. Serve hot with poached or baked white fish such as cod, haddock, or monkfish.

Makes about 2¾ cups
Serves 4-6

VARIATIONS: Use two 6oz cans white crabmeat in brine, drained and flaked, if fresh crabmeat is not available. Use chopped fresh parsley or chives in place of cilantro.

PEPPERED PARSLEY SAUCE

2oz fresh flat-leaf parsley
2 tablespoons pine nuts
1 clove garlic, crushed
¼ cup finely grated fresh Parmesan cheese
½ teaspoon cayenne pepper
½ teaspoon freshly ground black pepper
6 tablespoons olive oil
salt
squeeze of lemon juice (optional)

Put parsley, pine nuts, garlic, Parmesan, cayenne, black pepper, and 1 tablespoon of the oil in a small blender or food processor and blend to form a fairly smooth paste.

With the motor running, gradually add the remaining oil, pouring it in a steady stream through the feeder tube, until it is well incorporated.

Season to taste with salt and a squeeze of lemon juice, if liked. Add extra cayenne or black pepper, to taste, if liked. Serve with broiled or baked fish such as cod, salmon, or monkfish.

Makes about scant 1 cup
Serves 4-6

VARIATIONS: Use fresh basil in place of parsley. Use blanched almonds in place of pine nuts.

— SEAFOOD COCKTAIL SAUCE —

scant 1 cup mayonnaise (see page 30)
4 tablespoons extra-thick heavy cream
2 tablespoons tomato ketchup
1 teaspoon Worcestershire sauce
1 teaspoon lemon juice
few drops of Tabasco sauce
salt and freshly ground black pepper

Put the mayonnaise and cream in a bowl and beat together until smooth and well mixed.

Add the tomato ketchup, Worcestershire sauce, lemon juice, and Tabasco, and mix well.

Season to taste with salt and pepper. Serve with cooked cold seafood such as shrimp, scallops, or flaked crabmeat.

Makes about 1½ cups
Serves 4-6

VARIATIONS: Use lime juice in place of lemon juice. Add 2 teaspoons creamed horseradish sauce with the Tabasco sauce, if liked.

TARTAR SAUCE

2oz gherkins, drained
2 tablespoons capers, drained
generous 1 cup mayonnaise (see page 30)
4 tablespoons extra-thick heavy cream
1 tablespoon tarragon vinegar
1 tablespoon chopped fresh flat-leaf parsley
1 tablespoon chopped fresh chives
2 teaspoons chopped fresh tarragon
salt and freshly ground black pepper

Finely chop the gherkins and capers and place in a bowl.

Add the mayonnaise and mix well, then fold in the cream.

Stir in the vinegar and chopped herbs, mixing well. Season to taste with salt and pepper. Cover and leave in a cool place for about 30 minutes before serving, to allow the flavors to develop. Serve with broiled, baked, or poached fish such as cod or haddock.

Makes about 1¾ cups
Serves 8-10

VARIATION: Use white wine vinegar or lemon juice in place of tarragon vinegar.

PARSLEY & LEMON SAUCE

1¼ cups milk
1 shallot, cut in half
1 bay leaf
1 blade of mace
6 black peppercorns
1½ tablespoons butter
3 tablespoons all-purpose flour
scant ½ cup heavy cream
2 egg yolks
finely grated rind of 1 small lemon
3 tablespoons chopped fresh flat-leaf parsley
salt and freshly ground black pepper

Pour milk into a saucepan and add shallot, bay leaf, mace blade, and peppercorns.

Bring almost to a boil, then remove the pan from the heat, cover, and leave to infuse for 30 minutes. Strain into a bowl, reserving the milk and discarding the contents of the sieve. Put the butter in a small saucepan with the flour, cream, and infused milk. Heat gently, whisking continuously, until the sauce comes to a boil and is thickened and smooth. Simmer gently for 3-4 minutes, stirring. Remove the pan from the heat and gently whisk in the egg yolks.

Stir in the lemon rind and chopped parsley. Return to the heat and cook gently for 1-2 minutes longer, stirring all the time. Do not allow the sauce to boil. Season to taste with salt and pepper. Serve with cooked vegetables such as globe or Jerusalem artichokes, asparagus, green beans, or fava beans. This sauce is also good served with broiled fish.

Makes about 1¾ cups
Serves 4-6

CREAMED CURRY SAUCE

3 tablespoons butter
4 shallots, finely chopped
1 clove garlic, crushed
2 tablespoons all-purpose flour
3 tablespoons medium-hot curry paste
1 tablespoon tomato paste
1¼ cups vegetable stock (see page 15)
⅔ cup light cream
salt and freshly ground black pepper (optional)

Melt the butter in a small saucepan, add the shallots and cook gently for 8-10 minutes, stirring occasionally, until softened and lightly browned.

Add the garlic and cook for 1 minute. Add the flour and cook for 1 minute, stirring, then add the curry paste and tomato paste. Remove the pan from the heat and gradually whisk in the stock. Bring to a boil, whisking or stirring continuously, until the sauce thickens. Simmer gently for 2 minutes, stirring.

Add the cream and reheat gently until hot, stirring, but do not boil. Add salt and pepper to taste, if required. Serve with cooked vegetables such as cauliflower, green beans, or okra. This sauce is also good served with broiled or pan-fried chicken or turkey, or smoked haddock.

Makes about 2½ cups
Serves 4-6

VARIATION: Use 1 onion in place of shallots.

HERBY YOGURT SAUCE

scant 1 cup Greek-style yogurt
scant ½ cup plain yogurt
1 clove garlic, crushed
finely grated rind of 1 lime (optional)
2 tablespoons chopped fresh mixed herbs,
   such as parsley, chives, oregano, and mint
salt and freshly ground black pepper

Put the Greek-style yogurt and plain yogurt in a bowl and fold together to mix.

Add the garlic, lime rind, if using, and chopped herbs, and stir to mix well.

Season to taste with salt and pepper. Serve immediately with raw vegetables such as cherry tomatoes, carrots, or a mixed salad, or serve with lightly cooked cold vegetables such as green beans.

Makes about 1⅓ cups
Serves 4-6

VARIATIONS: Use 1-2 tablespoons chopped fresh mint in place of mixed herbs. Use finely grated rind of 1 small lemon in place of lime rind.

VOLUME 2

BROILED BELL-PEPPER SAUCE

4 red bell peppers
1 tablespoon olive oil
1 small red onion, finely chopped
1 stalk celery, finely chopped
1 clove garlic, crushed
²⁄₃ cup tomato juice
scant ½ cup vegetable stock (see page 15)
salt and freshly ground black pepper

Preheat the broiler to high. Cut bell peppers in half and place them cut-side down on the rack in a broiler pan. Broil for 10-15 minutes until skin is blackened and charred.

Remove from broiler and cover bell peppers with a clean damp dish towel. Set aside to cool. Once cool, remove skin, cores, and seeds from bell peppers and cut the flesh into chunks. Set aside. Heat oil in a saucepan, add onion, and celery, and cook gently for 8-10 minutes, stirring occasionally, until softened. Add bell-pepper flesh and garlic and cook for 1-2 minutes, stirring. Add the tomato juice, stock, and salt and pepper, and mix well. Bring to a boil, then reduce the heat, cover and cook gently for 15-20 minutes, stirring occasionally.

Remove pan from the heat, cool slightly, then purée mixture in a blender or food processor until smooth. Push purée through a sieve and discard contents of sieve. Reheat sauce gently or cool and chill before serving. Adjust seasoning to taste. Serve with cooked vegetables such as broccoli, cauliflower, or zucchini, or with a vegetable terrine. This sauce is also good served with broiled or baked chicken portions.

Makes about 1¾ cups
Serves 4-6

— SPINACH & NUTMEG SAUCE —

8oz fresh spinach leaves
2 tablespoons butter
3 shallots, finely chopped
1 clove garlic, crushed
scant ½ cup vegetable stock (see page 15)
2 bay leaves
1 sprig of thyme
4 tablespoons crème fraiche or heavy cream
½ teaspoon freshly grated nutmeg, or to taste
salt and freshly ground black pepper

Wash spinach thoroughly, shake dry, then remove and discard any tough stalks. Chop spinach roughly, then set aside.

Melt the butter in a saucepan, add shallots, and sauté for 5 minutes, stirring occasionally. Add garlic and sauté for 1 minute. Add spinach, stock, bay leaves, and sprig of thyme. Bring to a boil, then reduce the heat, cover, and cook gently for 10 minutes, stirring occasionally. Remove the pan from the heat and allow to cool slightly. Remove and discard bay leaves and thyme. Purée the mixture in a blender or food processor until smooth.

Return to the rinsed-out pan and stir in the crème fraiche or heavy cream. Reheat gently until hot, stirring. Season to taste with nutmeg, salt, and pepper. Serve with cooked vegetables such as carrots, baby corn, or new potatoes. This sauce is also good served with broiled or baked fish or chicken.

Makes about 2 cups
Serves 6

VARIATION: Use ground cumin in place of nutmeg.

TOMATO & CHILI SAUCE

3 tablespoons butter
1 leek, washed and finely chopped
1 small red bell pepper, seeded and finely chopped
1 clove garlic, crushed
2 fresh red chilies, cored, seeded, and finely chopped
1½ teaspoons ground cumin
1½ teaspoons ground coriander
14oz can chopped tomatoes
⅔ cup dry white wine
2 tablespoons tomato paste
salt and freshly ground black pepper

Melt butter in a saucepan, add leek, bell pepper, garlic, and chilies, and cook gently for 8-10 minutes, stirring, until softened.

Add ground spices and cook for 1 minute, stirring. Add chopped tomatoes with their juice, wine, tomato paste, and salt and pepper, and stir to mix. Bring to a boil, then reduce the heat, cover, and simmer for 10 minutes, stirring occasionally.

Uncover the pan, increase the heat slightly, and cook for a further 10-15 minutes, stirring occasionally, until the sauce has thickened. Check and adjust the seasoning. Serve with cooked or roast vegetables such as parsnips, Brussels sprouts, or zucchini. This sauce is also good served with hot pasta.

Makes about 3 cups
Serves 6

VARIATION: Use red wine or vegetable stock in place of white wine.

LEMON BUTTER

½ cup unsalted butter at room temperature
finely grated rind of 1 lemon
2 teaspoons fresh lemon juice
freshly ground black pepper

Place butter in a bowl and beat until softened. Add lemon rind, lemon juice, and black pepper to taste; beat until well mixed. Turn the flavored butter out on to a piece of plastic wrap and shape into a log. Wrap in the plastic wrap, then chill in the refrigerator for at least 1 hour before serving.

Cut into slices and serve on top of cooked fresh vegetables such as green beans, baby zucchini, or baby corn. Flavored butters are also ideal for serving on top of broiled meats, poultry, fish, or shellfish. They are delicious served with hot toast or warm fresh bread.

Serves 4-6

LIME BUTTER: use the finely grated rind of 1 lime and lime juice in place of lemon rind and juice.

HERB BUTTER: omit the lemon rind and juice and beat 2 tablespoons chopped fresh mixed herbs such as parsley, chives, and tarragon, into the softened butter with a squeeze of lemon juice.

GARLIC BUTTER: omit the lemon rind and beat 2 crushed cloves garlic and 2-3 teaspoons chopped fresh chives or parsley into the softened butter with the 2 teaspoons lemon juice.

ROAST TOMATO SAUCE

2lb cherry or baby plum tomatoes
1 tablespoon olive oil
1 red onion, finely chopped
2 cloves garlic, crushed
2 tablespoons sun-dried tomato paste
1 tablespoon chopped fresh oregano
salt and freshly ground black pepper

Preheat oven to 350F (180C). Arrange tomatoes in a single layer in a shallow ovenproof dish. Roast for 20 minutes or until soft. Remove from the oven and set aside to cool slightly, then purée in a blender or food processor until smooth.

Press the tomato paste through a sieve and discard the skins and seeds. Reserve the tomato sauce. Heat the oil in a saucepan, add the onion and garlic, and sauté for 6-8 minutes, or until softened. Add reserved tomato sauce, tomato paste, chopped oregano, and salt and pepper, and mix well. (If you prefer a smoother sauce, simply process all the ingredients in a small blender or food processor until thoroughly combined.)

Bring to a boil, then reduce the heat and simmer, uncovered, for 10 minutes, stirring occasionally. Adjust the seasoning and serve with cooked vegetables such as cauliflower or broccoli flowerets, boiled new potatoes, or roast vegetables. This sauce is also good served with broiled or baked chicken or fish.

Makes about 2¾ cups
Serves 4-6

VARIATION: Use 2-3 tablespoons chopped fresh basil in place of oregano.

PINEAPPLE SALSA

10oz prepared fresh pineapple
6 scallions
½ small yellow bell pepper, seeded
2 teaspoons finely grated, peeled fresh ginger root
1 tablespoon freshly squeezed orange juice
1 tablespoon olive oil
1 teaspoon honey
1 tablespoon chopped fresh cilantro
freshly ground black pepper

Finely chop the pineapple and place it in a bowl. Chop the scallions and finely chop the yellow bell pepper. Add to the pineapple and stir to mix.

Put the ginger, orange juice, olive oil, honey, and chopped cilantro in a separate small bowl and mix well. Pour the orange juice mixture over the chopped vegetables and pineapple and toss to mix well.

Season to taste with black pepper. Cover and leave to stand at room temperature for about 30 minutes before serving. Serve with broiled or grilled meat and poultry such as pork kabobs or chicken portions.

Serves 6

VARIATIONS: Use canned (drained) pineapple in place of fresh pineapple. Use red bell pepper in place of yellow bell pepper.

RED ONION SALSA

3 tomatoes
½ small red bell pepper, seeded
1 red onion
2 tablespoons tomato juice
1 tablespoon olive oil
2 teaspoons hot horseradish sauce
1 tablespoon chopped fresh flat-leaf parsley
salt and freshly ground black pepper

Using a sharp knife, cut a small cross in the blossom end of each tomato. Place the tomatoes in a bowl, cover with boiling water, and leave for about 30 seconds or until the skins split.

Remove using a slotted spoon and plunge into cold water, then drain well. Peel off the skins, then halve the tomatoes and remove and discard the seeds. Finely chop the flesh and place it in a bowl. Finely chop the red bell pepper and onion and add to the chopped tomato. Put the tomato juice, olive oil, horseradish sauce, and chopped parsley in a separate small bowl and mix well.

Add the tomato juice mixture to the chopped vegetables and toss to mix well. Season to taste with salt and pepper. Cover and leave to stand at room temperature for about 1 hour, to allow the flavors to develop. Serve with broiled, pan-fried, or roast meats such as beef or lamb steaks. This salsa is also good served with broiled or baked fish such as salmon.

Serves 4-6

MANGO & CILANTRO SALSA

2 ripe mangoes
2oz cucumber
4 scallions
1 tablespoon lime juice
3 tablespoons chopped fresh cilantro
freshly ground black pepper

Peel, pit, and finely chop the mangoes. Put the mango flesh in a bowl.

Finely chop the cucumber and scallions, and add to the mango flesh. Stir to mix.

Add the lime juice and chopped cilantro and mix well. Season to taste with black pepper. Cover and leave to stand at room temperature for about 1 hour before serving. Serve with pan-fried or oven-baked chicken or turkey portions.

Serves 4-6

VARIATIONS: Use lemon juice in place of lime juice. Use chopped fresh mint in place of cilantro.

FRESH TOMATO & CHILI SALSA

1lb plum tomatoes
2 shallots
1 fresh red or green chili, cored and seeded
1 clove garlic, crushed
2 sun-dried tomatoes in oil, drained and finely chopped
1 tablespoon olive oil
1 tablespoon chopped fresh oregano
salt and freshly ground black pepper

Using a sharp knife, cut a small cross in the blossom end of each tomato. Place the tomatoes in a bowl, cover with boiling water, and leave for about 30 seconds.

Remove using a slotted spoon and plunge into cold water, then drain well. Peel off the skins, then halve the tomatoes and remove and discard the seeds. Finely chop the flesh and place it in a bowl. Finely chop the shallots and chili. Add to the chopped tomatoes and stir to mix.

Add the garlic, sun-dried tomatoes, olive oil and oregano, and mix well. Season to taste with salt and pepper. Cover and leave to stand at room temperature for 1 hour before serving. Serve with broiled or baked fish such as red mullet, tuna, or salmon or with grilled chicken.

Serves 4

VARIATIONS: Use chopped fresh basil or cilantro in place of oregano. Add a few drops of Tabasco sauce if liked.

SPICED PEACH SALSA

3 ripe peaches
4 scallions
½ small yellow bell pepper, seeded
1 small fresh green chili, cored and seeded
juice of ½ lime
2 teaspoons medium-hot chili sauce
1 tablespoon chopped fresh cilantro
1 tablespoon chopped fresh mint
freshly ground black pepper

Peel, pit, and finely chop the peaches and place the chopped flesh in a bowl.

Finely chop the scallions and yellow bell pepper and add to the chopped peach. Finely chop the chili. Add the chili to the peach flesh and stir to mix well.

Add the lime juice, chili sauce, and chopped herbs, and mix well. Season to taste with black pepper. Cover and leave to stand at room temperature for at least 1 hour before serving. Serve with chargrilled tuna or salmon steaks, or grilled chicken or turkey portions. This salsa is also good served with cold cooked meats.

Serves 4-6

VARIATIONS: Use ripe nectarines in place of peaches.

TOMATO & GARLIC RELISH

2-3 beef tomatoes (total weight about 1lb 5oz)
2 tablespoons olive oil
1 teaspoon cumin seeds (optional)
1 small red onion, finely chopped
2 cloves garlic, crushed
2 teaspoons balsamic vinegar
1 teaspoon light brown sugar
2 tablespoons chopped fresh basil
salt and freshly ground black pepper

Preheat the broiler to high. Cut tomatoes in half and place them, cut-side down, on a foil-lined rack in a broiler pan. Grill the tomatoes until the skin is blistered and loose.

Remove from the broiler, cool slightly, then peel off and discard the skins. Remove or squeeze out and discard the seeds. Chop the flesh and set aside. Heat the oil in a small saucepan, add the cumin seeds, if using, and cook for 30 seconds, stirring. Add the onion and garlic, and sauté for 1-2 minutes. Add the tomato flesh and sauté gently for 4-5 minutes. If the tomatoes are especially juicy, sauté them over a high heat for a further 1-2 minutes, to reduce excess juice.

Remove the pan from the heat and stir in the balsamic vinegar, sugar, and chopped basil, mixing well. Season to taste with salt and pepper. Serve warm with broiled or grilled lamb, beef, chicken, or tuna, or cold cooked meats.

Serves 4-6

VARIATIONS: Use 1lb 5oz plum or standard tomatoes, cut in half, in place of beef tomatoes. Use 2-3 shallots in place of red onion.

TROPICAL FRUIT RELISH

8oz prepared fresh pineapple, finely chopped
1 ripe nectarine or peach, peeled, pitted, and finely chopped
1 ripe papaya, peeled, seeded, and finely chopped
1 small yellow bell pepper, seeded and finely chopped
1 tablespoon honey
1 tablespoon lime juice
2 tablespoons chopped fresh cilantro
freshly ground black pepper

Place the pineapple flesh in a bowl and add the chopped nectarine or peach, and chopped papaya.

Add the yellow bell pepper to the bowl and stir to mix well. In a separate small bowl, mix the honey and lime juice together. Drizzle over the chopped fruit.

Add chopped cilantro and toss to mix well. Season to taste with black pepper. Cover and leave to stand at room temperature for 30 minutes before serving. Serve with broiled fish such as monkfish, salmon, or swordfish, or chargrilled chicken or turkey portions. This relish is also good served with hot or cold baked ham.

Serves 6

VARIATION: Use ripe mango in place of pineapple.

V O L U M E 2

SUMMER CORN RELISH

4 scallions
8 red radishes
1 small red bell pepper
7oz can corn kernels, drained
1 tablespoon olive oil
2 teaspoons lemon juice
1 teaspoon Dijon mustard
2-3 tablespoons snipped fresh chives
salt and freshly ground black pepper

Chop the scallions and finely chop the radishes. Seed and finely chop the red bell pepper.

Place the chopped scallions, radishes, and red bell pepper in a bowl. Add the corn kernels and stir to mix. In a separate small bowl, mix together the olive oil, lemon juice, mustard, chives, and salt and pepper.

Pour over the corn mixture and toss well to mix. Cover and leave to stand at room temperature for about 30 minutes, before serving. Serve with broiled or grilled chicken or turkey portions or kabobs.

Serves 4-6

VARIATIONS: Use 1 small red onion in place of scallions. Use chopped fresh parsley or cilantro in place of chives.

BELL PEPPER & TOMATO RELISH

2 red bell peppers
1 yellow bell pepper
3 shallots, sliced
3 plum tomatoes, skinned, seeded, and chopped
1 clove garlic, crushed
⅓ cup pitted black olives, finely chopped
1 tablespoon olive oil (optional)
1 tablespoon chopped fresh basil
1 tablespoon chopped fresh flat-leaf parsley
salt and freshly ground black pepper

Preheat the broiler to high. Cut the bell peppers in half and place them cut-side down on the rack in a broiler pan.

Broil the bell peppers for 10-15 minutes until the skin is blackened and charred. Remove from the broiler and cover the peppers with a clean damp dish towel. Set aside to cool. Meanwhile, place the shallot slices on the rack in the broiler pan. Broil for about 5 minutes, turning once, until slightly softened. Remove from the broiler and cool. Remove the skin, cores, and seeds from the bell peppers and chop the flesh. Finely chop the shallots. Place the chopped bell pepper flesh, shallots, tomatoes, garlic, and olives in a bowl and stir to mix well.

Add the olive oil, if using, and chopped herbs and mix well. Season to taste with salt and pepper. Cover and set aside for about 1 hour before serving. Serve with broiled or pan-fried meat or poultry such as beef, pork, or chicken, or broiled fish such as lemon sole or plaice.

Serves 4-6

VARIATIONS: Use standard tomatoes in place of plum tomatoes. Use chopped fresh oregano or marjoram in place of basil.

SALSA VERDE

1 small onion
2 cloves garlic
4 tablespoons chopped fresh parsley
2 tablespoons chopped fresh mint
1 tablespoon snipped fresh chives
1 tablespoon capers, drained and chopped
4 tablespoons olive oil
2 tablespoons lemon juice
1 teaspoon Dijon mustard
few drops of Tabasco sauce, or to taste
salt and freshly ground black pepper

Peel and finely chop the onion. Peel and crush the garlic cloves.

Place the onion, garlic, chopped herbs, and capers in a small bowl and stir to mix. Add the olive oil, lemon juice, and mustard, and mix well. Add the Tabasco sauce, and salt and pepper to taste.

Cover and leave to stand at room temperature for about 30 minutes, to allow the flavors to develop. Serve with broiled meats such as lamb, pork, or beef steaks, or broiled fish such as haddock or monkfish.

Serves 4

VARIATIONS: Use lime juice in place of lemon juice. Omit the Tabasco sauce and add 1 finely chopped seeded fresh red or green chili to the salsa. Peel, pit, and finely chop 1 small avocado and add to the salsa, if liked.

ORIENTAL MARINADE

4 tablespoons orange juice
1 tablespoon olive oil
1 tablespoon dry sherry
1 tablespoon light soy sauce
1 tablespoon honey
2 tablespoons chopped fresh cilantro
2 teaspoons finely grated, peeled fresh ginger root
1 clove garlic, crushed
freshly ground black pepper

Put the orange juice, olive oil, sherry, soy sauce, honey, chopped cilantro, ginger, garlic, and black pepper in a non-metallic bowl or dish and mix together thoroughly.

Add poultry or meat to the marinade and turn to coat. Cover and leave to marinate in the refrigerator for 2-3 hours. If using fish, add to the marinade, turn to coat all over, then marinate for about 1 hour before cooking.

Remove the meat or fish from the marinade, reserving the marinade. Broil or grill the meat or fish until cooked, turning frequently and basting with the marinade during cooking, if liked. This marinade is enough to marinate about 1-1½lb poultry such as chicken or duck breast fillets, meat such as lamb cutlets, diced pork, or beef steaks, or fish such as monkfish, salmon, or seafood.

Makes about ⅔ cup
Serves 4-6

ROSEMARY & LEMON MARINADE

6 tablespoons olive oil
finely grated rind of 1 lemon
juice of 2 lemons
2 tablespoons finely chopped fresh rosemary
salt and freshly ground black pepper

Put the olive oil, lemon rind and juice, chopped rosemary, and salt and pepper in a non-metallic bowl or dish and mix together thoroughly.

Add poultry or meat to the marinade and turn to coat. Cover and leave to marinate in the refrigerator for 2-3 hours. If using fish, add to the marinade, turn to coat all over, then marinate for about 1 hour before cooking. Remove the meat or fish from the marinade, reserving the marinade.

Broil or grill the meat or fish until cooked, turning frequently and basting with the marinade during cooking, if liked. This is enough to marinate about 1-1½lb poultry such as chicken or turkey breast fillets, meat such as lamb cutlets, lamb or beef steaks, or kabobs, or fish such as monkfish, cod, or haddock. It is also ideal for marinating vegetables.

Makes about 1 cup
Serves 4-6

MUSTARD MARINADE

4 tablespoons dry white wine
1 tablespoon olive oil
juice of ½ lemon
1 tablespoon wholegrain mustard
1 tablespoon Dijon mustard
salt and freshly ground black pepper

Put the wine, olive oil, lemon juice, mustards, and salt and pepper in a non-metallic bowl or dish and mix together thoroughly.

Add poultry or meat to the marinade and turn to coat in the marinade. Cover and leave to marinate in the refrigerator for 2-3 hours. Remove the poultry or meat from the marinade, reserving the marinade. Broil or grill the poultry or meat until cooked, turning frequently and basting with the marinade during cooking, if liked.

This marinade is enough to marinate about 1-1½lb poultry such as chicken or turkey breast fillets, or meat such as lamb, pork, or beef steaks. It is also ideal for marinating chicken, meat, or vegetable kabobs.

Makes about ¾ cup
Serves 4-6

VARIATIONS: Use red wine or beer in place of white wine. Use juice of 1 lime in place of lemon juice.

TANDOORI PASTE

1 red onion, cut into quarters
2 cloves garlic, peeled and roughly chopped
1in piece fresh ginger root, peeled and roughly chopped
1 fresh red or green chili, cored, seeded, and chopped
juice of ½ lemon
1 tablespoon ground coriander
1 tablespoon ground cumin
2 teaspoons garam masala
1 teaspoon turmeric
1 teaspoon ground cinnamon
1 teaspoon olive oil
½ teaspoon each salt and freshly ground black pepper
2 tablespoons chopped fresh cilantro
scant 1 cup plain yogurt

Put the onion, garlic, ginger, chili, and lemon juice in a small blender or food processor and blend until finely chopped (see above). Add all the ground spices, the olive oil, salt, and pepper, and process to form a relatively smooth paste. Transfer the spice paste into a non-metallic bowl or dish, add the chopped cilantro and yogurt and mix well.

Add poultry or meat to the paste and turn to coat completely. Cover and marinate in the refrigerator for at least 4 hours, or overnight. Remove the poultry from the marinade. Discard leftover paste. Broil or grill poultry or meat until cooked, turning frequently and basting with melted ghee or oil during cooking, if liked. This paste is enough to marinate about 1½-2lb chicken or turkey portions or breast fillets.

Makes about 2 cups
Serves 6-8

TASTY BARBECUE PASTE

1 small onion
1 clove garlic
1 fresh red or green chili
2 tablespoons tomato paste
1 tablespoon olive oil
2 teaspoons red wine vinegar
2 teaspoons light brown sugar
1 teaspoon Worcestershire sauce
1 teaspoon Dijon mustard
few drops of Tabasco sauce
salt and freshly ground black pepper

Peel and chop the onion. Peel and crush the garlic clove, and seed and chop the chili.

Put the onion, garlic and chili in a small blender or food processor and process until finely chopped. Add the tomato paste, olive oil, vinegar, sugar, Worcestershire sauce, mustard, Tabasco sauce, and salt and pepper, and process to mix well. Transfer the barbecue paste into a non-metallic bowl or dish. Add the poultry or meat to the paste and turn to coat lightly. Alternatively, brush or spread the paste over the meat. Cover and marinate in the refrigerator for at least 4 hours, or overnight.

Remove the poultry or meat from the barbecue paste and scrape off most of the paste before cooking. Discard leftover paste. Broil or grill the poultry or meat until cooked, turning frequently and brushing lightly with oil during cooking, if liked. This paste is enough to marinate about 1lb poultry such as chicken or turkey portions or breast fillets, or meat such as beef steaks, or lamb chops.

Makes about ¾ cup
Serves 4

MOROCCAN PASTE

3 shallots
2 cloves garlic
2 tablespoons olive oil
2 tablespoons lime juice
1 teaspoon ground cumin
1 teaspoon ground coriander
1 teaspoon hot chili powder
½ teaspoon turmeric
¼ teaspoon ground cinnamon
2 tablespoons chopped fresh cilantro
salt and freshly ground black pepper

Roughly chop the shallots. Crush garlic cloves. Put in a small blender or food processor and process until finely chopped.

Add the olive oil, lime juice, ground spices, chopped cilantro, and salt and pepper, and process until thoroughly mixed to form a paste. Transfer the paste into a non-metallic bowl or dish. Add the meat or poultry to the paste and turn to coat lightly. Alternatively, brush or spread the paste over the meat. Cover and marinate in the refrigerator for at least 4 hours, or overnight. Remove the meat or poultry from the paste and scrape off most of the paste before cooking. Discard leftover paste.

Broil or grill the meat or poultry until cooked, turning frequently and brushing lightly with oil during cooking, if liked. This paste is enough to coat and marinate about 1lb meat such as lamb or beef kabobs, or steaks, or poultry such as chicken, turkey, or duck portions or breast fillets.

Makes about ⅔ cup
Serves 4

VARIATION: Use lemon juice in place of lime juice.

LIME & GINGER MARINADE

3 tablespoons olive oil
1 teaspoon sesame oil (optional)
finely grated rind of 1 lime
juice of 2 limes
1½in piece fresh ginger root, peeled and finely grated
1 clove garlic, crushed
salt and freshly ground black pepper

Put the olive oil, sesame oil, if using, lime rind and juice, ginger, garlic, and salt and pepper in a non-metallic bowl or dish and mix together thoroughly.

Add poultry or meat to the marinade and turn to coat. Cover and leave to marinate in the refrigerator for 2-3 hours. If using fish, add to the marinade, turn to coat all over, then marinate for about 1 hour before cooking. Remove the poultry, meat, or fish from the marinade, reserving the marinade.

Broil or grill the poultry, meat, or fish until cooked, turning frequently and basting with the marinade during cooking, if liked. This marinade is enough to marinate about 1-1½lb poultry such as chicken or turkey breast fillets, meat such as lamb cutlets, pork chops, or beef steaks, or white fish fillets such as cod, haddock, or plaice. It is also ideal for marinating chicken or meat kabobs.

Makes about ⅔ cup
Serves 4-6

CRÈME ANGLAISE

1¼ cups milk
1 vanilla bean, split in half lengthwise
3 egg yolks
1 tablespoon superfine sugar

Pour the milk into a small heavy-based saucepan, add the vanilla bean, and heat gently until almost boiling. Remove the pan from the heat and set aside to infuse for 15 minutes. Remove and discard the vanilla bean. Put the egg yolks and sugar in a bowl and whisk together until thick and creamy.

Gradually whisk in the hot infused milk, then strain back into the saucepan. Cook over a low heat, stirring continuously, for about 10 minutes, or until the mixture thickens enough to thinly coat the back of a wooden spoon. Do not allow the mixture to boil or it may curdle. Serve hot or cold.

If serving cold, pour the egg custard into a clean bowl and cover the surface closely with a piece of non-stick baking parchment, to prevent a skin forming, and allow to cool. Serve with broiled, baked, or stewed fruit, hot baked or steamed fruit puddings, or fruit cobblers.

Makes about 1½ cups
Serves 4

VARIATION: Infuse the milk with the pared rind of 1 lemon in place of vanilla bean.

BASIC SWEET WHITE SAUCE

5 teaspoons cornstarch
1¼ cups milk
knob of butter
5 teaspoons superfine sugar, or to taste

Put the cornstarch in a small bowl, add a little of the milk, and mix together until smooth. Heat the remaining milk in a small saucepan with the butter, until just boiling. Pour the hot milk on to the cornstarch mixture, stirring continuously. Return the mixture to the saucepan and bring slowly to a boil, stirring, until the sauce thickens.

Simmer gently for 2-3 minutes, stirring. Stir in the sugar to taste. Serve hot with fruit puddings, pies, and tarts.

Makes about 1¼ cups
Serves 4

LEMON/ORANGE SAUCE
Follow the recipe for Basic Sweet White Sauce. Stir in the finely grated rind of 1 lemon or 1 small orange just before serving.

QUICK VANILLA SAUCE
Follow the recipe for Basic Sweet White Sauce. Stir in ½-1 teaspoon vanilla extract, or to taste, just before serving.

QUICK CHOCOLATE SAUCE
Blend 3-4 teaspoons cocoa powder with 2 tablespoons of hot water until smooth, then set aside. Follow the recipe for Basic Sweet White Sauce. Once the sauce has thickened, stir in the cocoa paste and reheat gently until hot, stirring. Stir in sugar to taste and serve.

NECTARINE COULIS

4 ripe nectarines
2 tablespoons fresh orange juice
5 teaspoons superfine sugar, or to taste
2-3 teaspoons brandy, or to taste (optional)

Peel, halve, and pit the nectarines and roughly chop the flesh. Put nectarine flesh in a saucepan with orange juice and sugar. Heat gently, stirring, until sugar has dissolved. Bring slowly to a boil, then cover and simmer for 10-15 minutes or until the fruit is soft, stirring occasionally. Remove the pan from the heat and cool slightly.

Mash the fruit, then press the mixture through a nylon sieve into a bowl. Discard the contents of the sieve.

Stir the brandy, if using, into the nectarine coulis, then taste for sweetness and stir in more sugar, if necessary. Serve warm or cold with prepared fresh fruit such as strawberries or raspberries, crêpes or pancakes, iced desserts, or ice cream.

Makes about 1¼ cups
Serves 4-6

VARIATIONS: Use rum or orange-flavored liqueur such as Cointreau in place of brandy.

CHOCOLATE FUDGE SAUCE

6oz good quality plain chocolate
scant ½ cup heavy cream
⅓ cup light brown sugar
2 tablespoons corn syrup
1 tablespoon butter

Break the chocolate into squares. Place the chocolate, cream, sugar, corn syrup, and butter in a small heavy-based saucepan.

Heat gently, stirring, until the chocolate has melted and the sugar has dissolved. Bring slowly to a boil, stirring, then simmer very gently for 1-2 minutes, stirring occasionally.

Cool slightly before serving, then serve hot or warm with broiled or baked fruit, hot vanilla or chocolate sponge puddings or desserts, profiteroles, or ice cream.

Makes about 1⅓ cups
Serves 4-6

VOLUME 2

WHITE CHOCOLATE SAUCE

6oz white chocolate
⅔ cup heavy cream
1 tablespoon butter

Roughly chop the chocolate.

Put the chocolate, cream, and butter into a heatproof bowl. Place the bowl over a pan of simmering water.

Heat gently, stirring, until the ingredients have melted together and the sauce is well blended and smooth. Serve warm or at room temperature with raw or broiled fruit, hot sponge or baked puddings, or fruit tarts. If serving the sauce cold, stir it well before serving.

Makes about 1¼ cups
Serves 4-6

VARIATION: Use milk chocolate in place of white chocolate.

— BUTTERSCOTCH NUT SAUCE —

¾ cup chopped walnuts
3 tablespoons butter
¼ cup superfine sugar
1 tablespoon lemon juice
scant 1 cup heavy cream

Spread the walnuts out in a broiler pan then toast under the broiler for 2-3 minutes, turning frequently until lightly browned. Set aside to cool.

Put the butter in a small heavy pan and heat gently until melted. Add the sugar and cook, stirring, to a dark caramel. Remove from the heat and stir in 5 tablespoons hot water and the lemon juice. Take care when adding the water as the mixture may spit.

Return the pan to the heat and stir until smooth. Add the cream then cook gently, stirring, for 1-2 minutes to make a smooth sauce. Remove from the heat and stir in the walnuts. Serve with roast apples or pears, ice cream, or steamed puddings.

Makes about 2 cups
Serves 6-8

BLACK CHERRY SAUCE

8oz pitted black or dark red cherries
½ cinnamon stick
¼ cup superfine sugar, or to taste
2-3 teaspoons kirsch, or to taste
1 teaspoon cornstarch or arrowroot

Put the cherries and cinnamon stick in a small heavy saucepan with scant ½ cup water. Cover, bring slowly to a boil, then simmer gently, stirring occasionally, until the cherries are softened. Remove and discard the cinnamon stick.

Add sugar to taste, stirring until dissolved, then add the kirsch to taste. In a small bowl, blend the cornstarch or arrowroot with 1 tablespoon cold water, then stir the cornstarch or arrowroot mixture into the cherry sauce. (Add ½-1 teaspoon extra cornstarch or arrowroot if you prefer a slightly thicker sauce.)

Bring slowly to a boil, stirring, until the sauce thickens. Simmer gently for 2-3 minutes, stirring. Serve hot with steamed or baked sponge or chocolate puddings, pancakes, crêpes, or ice cream.

Makes about 1¼ cups
Serves 4

VARIATIONS: Use brandy in place of kirsch. Use light brown sugar in place of superfine sugar.

TANGY LEMON SAUCE

⅔ cup heavy cream
⅔ cup plain fromage frais (8% fat)
4 tablespoons good quality lemon curd
finely grated rind of 1 small lemon (optional)

Put the cream and fromage frais into a bowl and whip together until the mixture thickens and just holds its shape.

Fold in the lemon curd and lemon rind, if using, until well combined.

Serve with fresh fruit such as sliced strawberries or peaches, fresh fruit salad, or cold fruit tarts.

Serves 6-8

VARIATIONS: Use the finely grated rind of 1 lime and lime curd in place of lemon rind and lemon curd. Fold the lemon curd and lemon rind into 1¼ cups un-whipped crème fraîche, if liked.

STRAWBERRY-RHUBARB SAUCE

1⅔ cups strawberries
8oz rhubarb, trimmed
¼ cup butter
¼ cup superfine sugar, or to taste
1 tablespoon amaretto

Hull and halve the strawberries. Cut the rhubarb into ½-in pieces.

Put the strawberries and rhubarb into a saucepan with the butter and scant ½ cup water. Heat gently, stirring occasionally, until the mixture comes to a boil, then cover and simmer for about 10 minutes, until the rhubarb is soft. Remove the pan from the heat and cool slightly, then purée the mixture in a blender or food processor until smooth. Return the mixture to the rinsed-out pan.

Stir in sugar to taste, then reheat gently, stirring, until the sugar has dissolved. Bring slowly to a boil, stirring occasionally, then stir in the amaretto. Serve hot or cold with fruit pies, hot baked or sponge puddings, pancakes, creamy desserts, or ice cream.

Makes about 2½ cups
Serves 6

VARIATIONS: Use raspberries in place of strawberries. Use light soft brown sugar in place of superfine sugar.

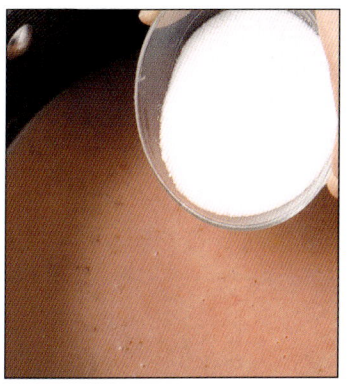

MOCHA CUSTARD

4 teaspoons custard mix
1 tablespoon light brown sugar
1¼ cups milk
1-2 teaspoons instant coffee granules, or to taste
2oz plain chocolate, broken into squares
few drops of vanilla extract (optional)

Put the custard mix in a small bowl with the sugar. Add a little of the milk and mix to form a smooth paste. Set aside. In a separate small bowl, dissolve the coffee granules in 1 tablespoon hot water.

Add the dissolved coffee to the custard paste and mix well. Set aside. Put the remaining milk in a small heavy saucepan, add the chocolate, and heat gently until the melted, stirring occasionally. Pour the hot chocolate milk on to the blended custard mixture, stirring continuously.

Return the mixture to the pan and heat gently, stirring continuously, until the custard sauce comes to a boil and thickens. Simmer gently for 1-2 minutes, stirring. Stir in the vanilla extract, if using. Serve hot with hot baked or steamed sponge puddings, or upside-down fruit puddings.

Makes about 1⅓ cups
Serves 4

VARIATION: Use 1 tablespoon superfine sugar in place of light brown sugar.

MELBA SAUCE

4 tablespoons red currant jelly
1⅔ cups raspberries
2 tablespoons confectioners' sugar, sifted
1 tablespoon framboise liqueur or kirsch, or to taste

Put the red currant jelly in a small saucepan and heat gently until melted. Remove the pan from the heat.

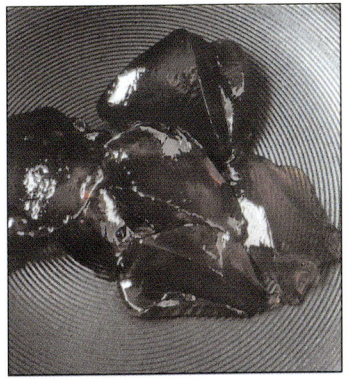

Put the raspberries in a small blender or food processor. Add the melted red currant jelly, confectioners' sugar, and framboise liqueur or kirsch, and blend to form a smooth purée.

Press the purée though a nylon sieve and discard the contents of the sieve. Pour the sauce into a sauceboat and serve with poached pears or peaches, meringues, or ice cream.

Makes about 1 cup
Serves 4

VARIATION: Use blackberries or loganberries in place of raspberries.

MARMALADE SAUCE

1 orange
5 tablespoons orange marmalade
2 teaspoons arrowroot
1-2 teaspoons brandy (optional)

Squeeze the juice from the orange. Pour the juice into a measuring cup and make up to ⅔ cup with cold water. Pour the mixed orange juice and water into a small saucepan.

Add the marmalade and stir to mix. Heat gently, stirring occasionally, until the marmalade has dissolved, then bring the mixture gently to a boil. In a small bowl, blend the arrowroot with 1 tablespoon of cold water. Pour the hot marmalade mixture on to the arrowroot mixture, stirring continuously. Return the mixture to the saucepan and bring slowly to a boil, stirring, until the sauce thickens.

Simmer gently for 1-2 minutes, stirring, then stir in the brandy, if using. Serve hot with steamed or baked sponge puddings, fruit puddings, or ice cream.

Makes about 1 cup
Serves 4

VARIATION: Use juice of 1 lemon and 1 lime, and lemon and lime marmalade, in place of orange juice and orange marmalade, and omit the brandy.

ORANGE & GINGER SAUCE

1 orange
4 pieces of preserved stem ginger in syrup, drained (about 2oz total weight)
2 teaspoons arrowroot
2 tablespoons light brown sugar
1 tablespoon ginger syrup from the jar of preserved stem ginger

Finely grate the rind from the orange and squeeze the juice. Finely chop the stem ginger. Set aside.

In a small bowl, blend the arrowroot with 1 tablespoon cold water. Set aside. Put the orange juice in a small heavy saucepan with the sugar and scant ½ cup water. Heat gently, stirring, until the sugar has dissolved, then bring to a boil. Pour the hot orange liquid on to the arrowroot mixture, stirring continuously.

Return the mixture to the saucepan and stir in the ginger syrup, orange rind, and chopped ginger. Bring slowly to a boil, stirring, until the sauce thickens, then simmer gently for 1-2 minutes, stirring. Serve hot with steamed or baked puddings, or fresh or dried fruit salads or compotes.

Makes about 1 cup
Serves 4

VARIATION: Use superfine sugar in place of light brown sugar.

RUM & RAISIN SAUCE

⅓ cup raisins
1 tablespoon cornstarch
scant 1 cup milk
scant ½ cup heavy cream
1 tablespoon butter
1 tablespoon light brown sugar
2 tablespoons rum

Roughly chop the raisins, then set aside. In a small bowl, blend the cornstarch with 2 tablespoons of the milk until smooth. Set aside.

Heat the remaining milk, the cream, and butter in a small heavy saucepan, until almost boiling. Pour the hot milk and cream mixture on to the cornstarch mixture, stirring continuously. Return the mixture to the saucepan and bring slowly to a boil, stirring, until the sauce thickens. Simmer gently for 2-3 minutes, stirring.

Stir in the sugar, rum, and chopped raisins and reheat gently until hot. Serve hot with pancakes, crêpes, sponge puddings, or ice cream.

Makes about 1⅔ cups
Serves 4

VARIATIONS: Use chopped ready-to-eat dried prunes, apricots, figs, or sultanas in place of raisins. Use milk in place of heavy cream.

FOREST FRUIT COULIS

12oz mixed prepared fresh berries such as raspberries, strawberries, blackberries, black currants, and red currants
¼ cup superfine sugar, or to taste
2-3 teaspoons crème de cassis, or to taste

Place the mixed berries in a saucepan with the sugar and 2 tablespoons water. Heat gently, stirring, until the sugar has dissolved. Bring slowly to a boil, then cover the pan and cook gently for 10-15 minutes, or until the fruit is pulpy, stirring occasionally.

Remove the pan from the heat, cool slightly, then press the pulp and juice through a nylon sieve. Discard the contents of the sieve.

Stir the crème de cassis into the fruit coulis, then taste for sweetness and stir in more sugar and crème de cassis, if necessary. Serve warm or cold with fresh fruit tartlets, crêpes or pancakes, yogurt ice, or ice cream.

Makes about 1¼ cups
Serves 4-6

VARIATION: Use other fruit-flavored liqueurs, such as cherry or framboise liqueur, or sloe gin in place of crème de cassis.

RASPBERRY COULIS

1⅔ cups raspberries
1 tablespoon confectioners' sugar, sifted, or to taste
2 teaspoons framboise liqueur or kirsch, or to taste (optional)

Put the raspberries in a small blender or food processor and blend to form a purée.

Press the raspberry purée through a nylon sieve into a bowl to remove the seeds. Discard the seeds.

Add confectioners' sugar to the raspberry coulis to taste, stirring to mix well. Stir in the framboise liqueur or kirsch, if using. Serve cold with creamy cold desserts, fresh fruit, ice creams, sorbets, or yogurt ices.

Makes about ¾ cup
Serves 4

VARIATIONS: Use blackberries or strawberries in place of raspberries and add confectioners' sugar and liqueur to taste. Use frozen (defrosted) raspberries in place of fresh.

APRICOT & CINNAMON COULIS

14oz can apricot halves in juice
1 teaspoon ground cinnamon
2 tablespoons confectioners' sugar, sifted
2 teaspoons amaretto (optional)

Put the apricots and their juice in a small blender or food processor and blend until smooth. Add the cinnamon and blend until well mixed.

Press the apricot purée through a nylon sieve into a bowl. Discard the contents of the sieve.

Whisk or fold the confectioners' sugar into the apricot coulis until well mixed. Stir in the amaretto, if using. Serve with cold creamy desserts, fruit desserts, or ice cream.

Makes about 1¼ cups
Serves 4-6

VARIATIONS: Use canned peaches in place of apricots. Use ¼-½ teaspoon almond extract or to taste, in place of amaretto, if liked.

INDEX

Aioli, 28
Apricot and cinnamon coulis, 95
Arugula pesto, 29
Avocado sauce, 48
Barbecue sauce, 25
Basic sweet white sauce, 80
Basic white sauce, 16
Béchamel sauce, 18
Bell pepper and tomato relish, 70
Beurre blanc, 22
Black cherry sauce, 85
Blended white sauce, 16
Blue cheese sauce, 33
Broiled bell-pepper sauce, 57
Butterscotch nut sauce, 84
Cheese (Mornay) sauce, 17
Chicken stock, 12
Chocolate fudge sauce, 82
Cilantro pesto, 29
Classic pesto, 29
Creamed curry sauce, 55
Creamy artichoke sauce, 38
Creamy crab sauce, 50
Creamy mushroom sauce, 46
Crème Anglaise, 79
Curried mayonnaise, 31
Dill and mustard sauce, 47
Egg custard, see Crème Anglaise
Espagnole (brown) sauce, 20
Fish stock, 14
Forest fruit coulis, 93
Fresh cranberry sauce, 26
Fresh tomato and chili sauce, 65
Garlic butter, 60

Garlic and herb mayonnaise, 31
Green peppercorn sauce, 42
Herb butter, 60
Herby yogurt sauce, 56
Hollandaise, 24
Horseradish cream, 34
Horseradish mayonnaise, 31
Lemon butter, 60
Lemon caper sauce, 36
Lemon mayonnaise, 31
Lemon sauce, 80
Lime butter, 60
Lime and ginger marinade, 78
Mango and cilantro salsa, 64
Marmalade sauce, 90
Mayonnaise, 30
Mayonnaise variations, 31
Meat stock, 13
Melba sauce, 89
Mint sauce, 27
Mocha custard, 88
Moroccan paste, 77
Mustard marinade, 74
Mustard mayonnaise, 31
Nectarine coulis, 81
Onion sauce, 17
Orange sauce, 80
Orange and ginger sauce, 91
Oriental marinade, 72
Parsley sauce, 17
Parsley and lemon sauce, 54
Peanut satay sauce, 39
Peppered parsley sauce, 51
Pineapple salsa, 62
Plum and ginger sauce, 41
Quick chocolate sauce, 80
Quick tomato sauce, 19

Quick vanilla sauce, 80
Raspberry coulis, 94
Red onion salsa, 63
Red pesto, 29
Red wine (Burgundy) sauce, 37
Rémoulade sauce, 21
Roast tomato sauce, 61
Rosemary and lemon marinade, 73
Rum and raisin sauce, 92
Salsa verde, 71
Seafood cocktail sauce, 52
Spiced peach salsa, 66
Spicy Thai dipping sauce, 43
Spinach and nutmeg sauce, 58
Strawberry-rhubarb sauce, 87
Summer corn relish, 69
Tandoori paste, 75
Tangy lemon sauce, 86
Tarragon sauce, 40
Tartare sauce, 53
Tasty barbecue paste, 76
Tomato and basil sauce, 44
Tomato and chili sauce, 59
Tomato, onion, and garlic relish, 67
Traditional gravy, 32
Tropical fruit relish, 68
Vegetable stock, 15
Velouté sauce, 23
Watercress sauce, 45
White chocolate sauce, 83
White sauce variations, 17
White wine sauce, 49
Wild mushroom sauce, 35